First Facts®

# MY FIRST GUIDE TO

# FAST VEHICLES

by Nikki Potts

CAPSTONE PRESS
a capstone imprint

First Facts are published by Capstone Press,
1710 Roe Crest Drive, North Mankato, Minnesota 56003
www.mycapstone.com

**Library of Congress Cataloging-in-Publication Data**
Cataloging-in-publication data is available on the Library of Congress website.
ISBN 978-1-5157-3594-6 (library binding)
ISBN 978-1-5157-3601-1 (eBook PDF)

**Editorial Credits**
Carrie Sheely and Nikki Potts, editors; Kazuko Collins, designer; Jo Miller, media researcher; Katy LaVigne, production specialist

**Photo Credits**
Alamy: Henry Westheim Photography, 11, Jim West, 13, Tony Watson, 15; Dreamstime: Digitalstormcinema, cover (race car), Mksdphotos, 17 (top); Getty Images: David Madison, 5 (top); Newscom: Icon Sportswire/Marc Sanchez, 17 (bottom); Science Source: Cody Images, 5 (bottom); Shutterstock: i4lcocl2, 7 (top), Natursports, 19, Phil Lowe, 9, Rob Byron, cover (helicopter), Sibuet Benjamin, 21, Vytautas Kielaitis, 7, (bottom)

**Design Elements**
Shutterstock: Sergio Hayashi, graphixmania, Motorama, Jiri Vaclavek, Saint A

Printed and bound in China.
007874

# Table of Contents

# Land-speed Racers

From high-speed trains to helicopters, fast vehicles are breaking records all over the world. Once a record is broken, a new goal is set to break it again!

Every year racers try to break land-speed records. Vehicles that break these records can be considered the fastest in the world on land. The Thrust SSC set the current official land-speed record at 763.035 miles (1,227.986 kilometers) per hour in 1997.

## FACT

The Federation Internationale de l'Automobile (FIA) recognizes official land-speed records. The car must make two passes within one hour of each other. The official speed is the average of the two passes.

Thrust SSC in the Black Rock Desert in Nevada

Thrust SSC driver Andy Green sets a new land-speed record in 1997.

# ATVs

ATVs are made to drive on all types of terrain. Sometimes they have special tires. Paddle tires are used for riding through **dunes**. Studded tires help ATVs ride on ice.

Some ATV riders compete in races. They go up and down hills and make tight turns. Drivers shift their body weight during a race to stay balanced. An ATV's top speed is about 80 miles (129 km) per hour.

**dune**—a hill or ridge of sand piled up by the wind

**Lithuanian Open Motocross Championship**

# Helicopters

Large rotor blades lift helicopters into the air. Small tail rotors help them turn. Helicopters can fly forward, backward, up, down, and sideways. The Eurocopter X3 is the fastest helicopter in the world. It has a record speed of 293 miles (472 km) per hour.

People often use helicopters for rescue missions. The U.S. Coast Guard frequently uses the Jayhawk. It has a top speed of 207 miles (333 km) per hour.

**FACT**

The U.S. president travels on a helicopter called Marine One.

**MH-60T Jayhawk**

# High-speed Trains

High-speed trains take riders from one city to another. They run on electricity. Special tracks help them move quickly. Maglev trains use **magnets** to float above the track. The Shanghai Maglev train in China travels at 268 miles (431 km) per hour. It is the fastest train in the world.

**magnet**—a piece of metal that attracts iron or steel

Maglev train in Shanghai, China

**FACT**
Japan's high-speed trains are called bullet trains. The E5 and E6 bullet trains can go 200 miles (322 km) per hour.

# Hydroplanes

Hydroplanes are like airplanes on water. They skim over the water and look like they are flying. The **hulls** are designed to help the hydroplanes easily lift out of the water.

Hydroplane racing takes place on rivers and lakes. Unlimited hydroplanes are the fastest race boats in the world. Their **turbine**-powered engines help them hit speeds of more than 220 miles (354 km) per hour.

**hull**—the main body of a boat

**turbine**—an engine powered by steam or gas; the steam or gas moves through the blades of a fanlike device and makes it turn

Hydroplanes race at the Gold Cup Hydroplane Races on the Detroit River in 2005.

**FACT**

The first hydroplanes used engines from World War II (1939–1945) fighter jets.

# Sport Bikes

Sport bikes are high-performance **production** motorcycles designed for **paved** roads. Their powerful engines and lightweight **frames** are built for speed. The Hayabusa is one of the fastest sport bikes in the world. It can reach a speed of at least 186 miles (299 km) per hour.

**production**—produced in large amounts for the public to buy

**paved**—when a road or sidewalk is covered with a hard material, such as concrete or asphalt

**frame**—the main body of a bike

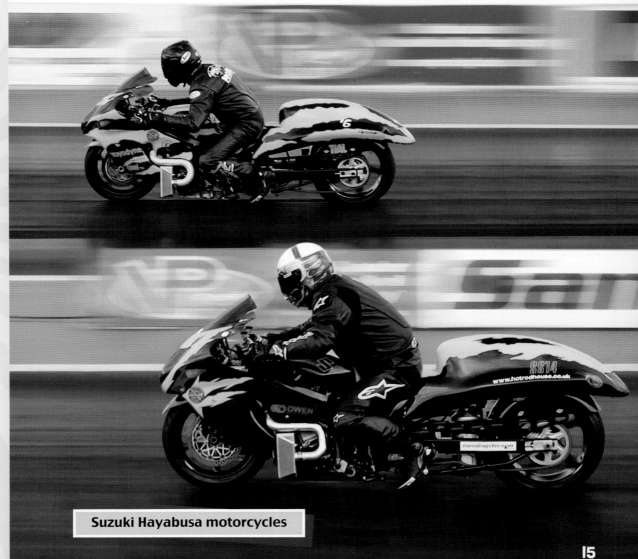

Suzuki Hayabusa motorcycles

# Dragsters

Dragsters race on short, straight tracks. The tracks are usually ⅛-mile (0.2-km) or ¼-mile (0.4-km) strips.

There are three main classes of dragsters in pro drag racing. They are top fuelers, pro stock cars, and funny cars. Of these types, top fuelers are the fastest. They reach speeds of more than 350 miles (563 km) per hour.

## FACT

Top fuelers have narrow frames with wheels that stick out. Funny cars and pro stock cars look more like factory-made cars.

pro stock cars

pro stock cars

top fuelers

# Open-wheel Race Cars

All race cars are built for speed. But **open-wheel** race cars, like Indy and Formula One (F1), are faster than cars that have a full body. They also have front and rear wings that push air down on the cars. This helps them grip the track.

Racers often drive open-wheel race cars on twisty, paved tracks. Indy cars reach speeds of 230 miles (370 km) per hour. F1 cars can reach speeds of 257 miles (414 km) per hour.

**open-wheel**—a race car built with the wheels outside of the main body

# Supercars

Supercars are **sports cars** that are designed for speed. They are made to drive on public roads. Like race cars, their body design is **aerodynamic**.

Most supercar engines use **turbochargers**. They boost the power of an engine without adding a lot of weight. Some supercars reach speeds up to 250 miles (402 km) per hour. Some of the top manufacturers of supercars include Ferrari, Lamborghini, Bugatti, and McLaren.

**sports car**—a low, small car that usually seats two people

**aerodynamic**—built to move easily through the air

**turbocharger**—a system that forces air through an engine to make a car go faster

**Bugatti Veyron 16.4 Grand Sport**

Supercars are rare and expensive. Only a limited number are produced. Most supercars cost between $350,000 and $5 million.

# Glossary

**aerodynamic** (air-oh-dye-NA-mik)—built to move easily through the air

**dune** (DOON)—a hill or ridge of sand piled up by the wind

**frame** (FRAYM)—the main body of a bike

**hull** (HUHL)—the main body of a boat

**magnet** (MAG-nit)—a piece of metal that attracts iron or steel

**open-wheel** (OH-puhn WEEL)—a race car built with the wheels outside of the main body

**paved** (PAYVED)—when a road or sidewalk is covered with a hard material, such as concrete or asphalt

**production** (pruh-DUHK-shuhn)—produced in large amounts for the public to buy

**sports car** (SPORTS KAHR)—a low, small car that usually seats two people

**turbine** (TUR-bine)—an engine powered by steam or gas; the steam or gas moves through the blades of a fanlike device and makes it turn

**turbocharger** (TUR-boh-char-juhr)—a system that forces air through an engine to make a car go faster

# Read More

**Nelson, Drew.** *Armored Vehicles.* Military Machines. New York: Gareth Stevens Pub., 2013.

**Polydoros, Lori.** *Drag Racing.* Super Speed. Mankato, Minn.: Capstone Press, 2013.

**Woods, Bob.** *Smokin' Sports Cars.* Fast Wheels! Berkeley Heights, N.J.: Enslow Publishers, Inc., 2013.

# Internet Sites

FactHound offers a safe, fun way to find Internet sites related to this book. All of the sites on FactHound have been researched by our staff.

Here's all you do:

Visit *www.facthound.com*

Type in this code: 9781515735946

Check out projects, games and lots more at
**www.capstonekids.com**

# Critical Thinking Using the Common Core

1. How is an official land-speed record determined? (Key Ideas and Details)

2. Many supercar engines use turbochargers. What is a turbocharger? (Craft and Structure)

# Index